We Should All Be Millionaires

How to Acquire Money,Earn,and Get Influence as a Woman

by

Jesica D. Bair

Table of contents

Introduction

When you're still a young adult, it's the best time to start saving money.

This is because your assets need time, decades to grow. Furthermore, you might have more money available now than later in life when you have more financial obligations.

If you follow the appropriate steps, building wealth is less complicated. Creating wealth is a desire that many individuals have, yet it can frequently seem like an impossible endeavor. Refrain from being seduced by get-rich-quick schemes and too-good-to-be-true offers that can lead you down a dangerous path since achieving this objective requires patience, perseverance, and discipline.

Do you wish to amass a fortune that would last throughout your life and provide

enough for your loved ones after passing? Most of us have this desire, but we rarely fulfill it, and when we are older, we lament the opportunities we lost.
The good news is that everyone may accumulate wealth over time by using specific guidelines and tactics. And the sooner you begin implementing these, the higher your likelihood of success.

Chapter 1

Why it is necessary to make Money

When you consider the price of daily requirements, you can see how important money is. Even though money can't buy happiness, being financially stable is crucial to take care of your family's essential needs.

You've probably heard someone declare they don't care about money at some point in your life, and you might have even said it yourself. Although this emotion seems good in theory, you shouldn't undervalue the value of money in real life, for better or ill.

Money can purchase protection and safety for you and your loved ones, but it cannot buy happiness. Humans require cash to pay for everything that makes life possible, including housing, food, medical expenses, and quality education. Although you won't need to be Bill Gates or have a large sum to pay for these items, you will require some money until you pass away.

Knowing about personal finance is crucial since you need money to buy the necessary supplies and services to survive. To ensure you'll still have enough when you can't exchange your labor for cash, you need to be frugal with the money you make and save enough for the future.

The earlier you begin saving, the more probable you will never experience financial difficulty or a shortage of funds. If you save enough money and make smart investments, you may achieve financial freedom, which is achieved when you have enough money to support yourself for the rest of your life.

The fact that the desire for money has been labeled as "the root of all evil" is one reason so many individuals claim not to care about money.

Indeed, materialistic people often let their concern with money push them to misbehave for their financial advantage. But money is merely a means of transaction in reality.

With money, exchanging your labor for a wide range of goods and services is simpler. The following are some topics to consider when it comes to the worth and significance of money.

Without money, acquiring food would require finding someone who possessed it and was prepared to barter it for a service you could render or a good you could manufacture. These types of bartering exchanges are time-consuming, ineffective, and less reliable ways to acquire the goods you require.
You no longer have to rely on other people to provide you with what you need in exchange for something they wish to trade

with you because of money. Since everyone agrees that money is worth it, you can exchange it for any goods or services you require. This improves market liquidity, which is the ease with which assets can be bought or sold.

This only applies when money has an enduring value, which derives from being a limited resource. The funds would lose all weight if it were possible for everyone to print as much as they want.

A centralized authority must ensure money's availability is constrained to protect its genuine value. In many instances, a central bank like the U.S. Federal Reserve regulates the money supply to prevent inflation, whereby there is an abundance of money that no longer has value.

Money's advantages

You may exchange your effort for goods you value thanks to the availability of money. Money has a variety of significant advantages, some of which are listed below:

- Freedom is a gift of money. With sufficient funds, you can live anywhere, fulfill your requirements, and indulge your interests. You'll experience even more freedom if you can achieve financial independence and have enough money to support yourself without working because you'll have more time to pursue your interests.
- You can follow your dreams when you have money. If you have money, you can establish a business, create the home of your dreams, support your family financially, and pursue

other objectives to improve your quality of life.

- Security is provided by money.
  When you have enough money saved up, you won't ever have to worry about paying for a place to live, enough food to eat, or being able to visit a doctor when you're sick. Even if you can't afford everything you desire, you'll still be able to lead a secure middle-class life.
- Money allows you to provide for your family more.
  Although passing down riches to the next generation might be advantageous, there is a narrow line between giving your kids money and teaching them healthy habits like hard work and morals.
- But money is essential since it enables you to give your family

access to better healthcare, educational prospects, and general life chances.

- There are many spoilt kids, leading to their inflated financial aspirations as they grow up. Yet, the trick will be to not give them every little luxury without effort and instead teach them about money.

Although money cannot purchase happiness, independence, stability, and the ability to follow your aspirations can contribute significantly to your satisfaction. Work hard, earn money, and learn how to start saving and invest it since that's why it's so crucial. As you begin investing your money, it works for you and spurs more productivity; eventually, you should have enough to retire.

Chapter 2

What constitutes a millionaire?

Consider a millionaire for a moment.
Think about something.
Does your idea of a millionaire owning a
large home, an expensive car, and fancy

clothing? That person might not be a millionaire, albeit they might be.

The mortgage lender may be the homeowner, the bank may be the vehicle owner, and they may have racked up a sizable credit card debt by making clothing purchases. While someone may appear to have it all, they might only be one mistake away from losing it all. People hold a variety of absurd misconceptions about millionaires in high regard. Asking ten unrelated strangers on the street about being a millionaire would elicit ten different responses. Most of them would be mistaken, too!

Let's get to the real meaning of being a millionaire by cutting through the nonsense.

What Does a Millionaire Mean?

A person with a million-dollar net worth is considered a millionaire. The calculation is straightforward math depending on your net worth. You are a millionaire if the sum of your assets and liabilities exceeds one million dollars.

Becoming a millionaire has nothing to do with your yearly income, feelings or emotions, or the judgment of your eccentric uncle. Again, it's a mathematical formula, and it doesn't give a damn about anyone else's or your feelings.

As an illustration, let's say you have $200,000 in liabilities and $1,400,000 in assets. Your net worth would be $1.2 million in that situation, making you a millionaire.

We can determine if someone has a net worth of at least $1 million by examining their balance sheet and considering their assets and debts. Let's say John Gate possesses the following possessions:

House: $450,000
Car: $20,000
$700,000 set aside for retirement
Investing: $90,000
Investments: $100,000
Other non-liquid assets' resale value: $20,000.
Cash: $20,000
Purchases in total: $1,400,000

Consider that John Gate is also liable for the following:

Loan amount: $220,000
$10,000 for a car loan
Liabilities totaling $230,000
John Doe is a millionaire based on the formula for estimating net worth, which is

what you own minus what you owe. John has assets of $1.4 million and liabilities of $230,000. Thus, his total net worth is $1,170,000 (assets fewer obligations). John is now a millionaire.

Chapter 3

Is it possible for everyone to become rich?

Although it may seem difficult to some, it doesn't have to be an unattainable fantasy. By retiring, you can easily make a million dollars with careful planning, persistence, and wise savings.

The Six Steps to Millionairedom.

You don't need a six-figure job or family wealth to become a millionaire. Instead, you should begin saving early and budget your money carefully. Here are some suggestions for preserving the million dollars you'll need for a luxurious or early retirement.

1. Start your savings early.

Starting early is the key to building your savings. By doing this, you can benefit from compounding's power. I'll assume you're 20 years old. If you made annual contributions of $6,000 ($500 per month) to an IRA for 40 years, your total investment would be $240,000.

Yet, assuming a 7% return, the power of compounding would cause your investment to increase to over $1.37 million. And if you saved $500 a month, you'd be a billionaire by the time you were 57.

2. Refrain from needless spending and debt
Put an end to your shopping sprees. Before tapping your card, consider the following:

Is this something I need?
"Do I already have something like this?"
Is this something I desire more than being a millionaire?
Spending money on things you don't need takes money away from investments.
Here's a dose of reality. For the same 40 years, investing an additional $25 a week would result in earnings of $277,693.
Can you eliminate $25 in wasteful spending from your weekly budget?
Perhaps, perhaps not. But if you can, it

will significantly assist you in achieving your objective.

3. Save 15% or more of your income.
The personal savings rate is the percentage of income left over after expenses and taxes. The Bureau of Economic Analysis figures show the rate fell to 2.3% in October 2022. (BEA).
Experts say more is needed for retirement savings and those aiming to become millionaires.

What amount should you preserve specifically? Although there is no right or wrong answer here, most financial advisors agree that if you want to build a nest egg for retirement, you should save at least 15% of your annual gross income, depending on your age. Although this amount may be out of reach for many, it is not. If your employer matches up to 6% of your salary in savings, you must save only 9% of your income.

4. Earn more cash

This is easier said than done, to be sure. Becoming a billionaire will be challenging if you can't save 15% of your income. But you do have a few choices, including:

requesting a wage raise (if you believe you are owed one)
putting in longer hours
hiring a second employee
increasing your income potential by getting training

In the long term, further training pays off the most. Assume you hold a license as a practical nurse (LPN). In 2021, the median annual income will be $48,070.

On the other hand, registered nurses make roughly $77,600 annually, which is almost $30,000 more. Of course, becoming an RN takes one to three more years.

But if one of your financial objectives is to become a millionaire, that extra cash each year can help you achieve it.

5. Refuse to Cultivate Lifestyle Inflation
This is called lifestyle inflation when you spend more money simply because you have more money. Suppose you pay $1,000 monthly to live in a cozy apartment in a great neighborhood. You move to a better apartment that costs $1,500 monthly after receiving a raise at work. Did you require a move?

Avoid caving to lifestyle inflation if you want to become a millionaire. Spend less simply because you can and put more money into savings and investments. You'll achieve your monetary objectives far more quickly.

6. Seek Assistance If You Need It

Retirement planning may be highly stressful, partly because there are so many investment options and so many unknowables ahead of you. Up to 60% of persons in the workforce admitted to having anxiety about retirement preparation. Only 25% of Americans feel confident they are taking the necessary steps to prepare for retirement.

That is why seeking professional assistance is so crucial. Among Americans, only 29% claimed they work with a financial advisor, while 65% stated they receive no financial guidance.

Working with a certified financial advisor is worthwhile unless you're an economic rock star.

Chapter 4

Why women make poor decisions.

"Many of the traits that define women as being particularly feminine are also the same behaviors that prohibit them from achieving financial independence."

Being financially illiterate is neither an insult to women nor anything to be embarrassed by. Perhaps because of their feminine character, some women tend to repeat the same financial blunders.

For these reasons, some women handle money poorly.

1. Merging love and money.
Many women enjoy providing financial assistance to others as one of their many rescue methods. Many women offer money freely when someone begs for a loan, often to their detriment. I virtually always see women suing the men they love for not repaying loans when I watch Judge Marilyn Milian on television. Allowing their relationships and their feelings to influence their financial decisions is a mistake women make.

If someone you care about asks or needs money, think of additional ways to aid him outside of just giving or lending him money. Assistance with drafting a résumé, networking, meal preparation, child care, and office work. Always prepare a contract before lending money. Discover how to stop putting other people's needs or wants ahead of your future.

2. Not negotiating before making a large or small purchase.
According to Frankel, women don't receive as much as males do because they don't ask for it and because asking makes them anxious. Women regard bargaining as intimidating, whereas men find it thrilling and engaging. Women don't get as much for their money, which does not imply that they are "bad" with money.

What large purchase or financial deal do you have coming up soon? Be prepared when negotiating with a car salesperson, getting a promotion at work, or deciding how much money you and your husband should spend on your upcoming vacation.

3. Failure to obtain written agreements for contracts, loans, and purchases
A contract that specifies the specifics of a sale, job offer, divorce settlement, family property partition, or service contract is another money error women make. If you need help managing your finances, it could be because you need to approach your purchases or financial dealings professionally.
Ensure that all financial transactions are done in writing and with the consent of all parties. Use file folders to manage your

receipts, contracts, financial agreements, payments, and other financial documents.

4. Not making efforts to achieve financial independence "If you're not saving the money you need to be financially independent, ask yourself why," Men are prepared to win at all costs. Women make a costly error when they "play like girls." Walking away with a lot of money is not wrong, unlawful, or unethical.

5. Permitting social pressure to have an impact on financial decisions
According to Frankel, one of the biggest financial blunders I've ever made was giving in to pressure to pay more than I wanted for group gifts.
We might overspend because of social pressure. For instance, knowing that others would also spend $100 on a baby shower

gift may cause you to spend ten times as much as you intended to. Because it affects their financial judgments, this can make women lousy with money.

6. Opting for financial planners without doing any research at all!
Women make financial mistakes like not employing a financial planner. But another money error that women frequently make that might ruin their financial situation is too trusting the wrong person with their finances. Refrain from blindly relying on anyone to manage your investment portfolio, whether your spouse, kids, relatives, or your best friend's stockbroker. Ask for a free consultation when interviewing potential investment brokers, check out their fees, and choose someone with a wide range of experience.

Chapter 5

Money making techniques

Why do some people seem to be able to draw money while others seem to reject it quickly?

Do those with money have access to information that the rest of us don't? What's their trick?

If you're like most individuals, one of your life goals is undoubtedly to become financially independent. But the route to wealth can sometimes seem obscure. You continue to work, pay your bills, and live paycheck to paycheck, much like a hamster on a wheel.

What if I told you that things could be different? What if I told you you could start attracting extra money into your life immediately? What if I also said you might achieve financial security by following these seven easy steps?

How to Attract Wealth: 7 Steps

1. Consider yourself deserving of happiness
It would help if you consider yourself deserving of happiness to attract prosperity. You'll note that I did not imply you had a right to happiness. The key word here is deserving. Our self-perception, which our morning ritual may significantly bolster, is the key to developing happiness.
Before you sincerely feel you deserve happiness, you cannot take any other

actions listed here. It would help to let go of the guilt and shame derived from the past for this to occur.

2. Pay attention to what you have right now.
Many people get caught up dwelling on what they lack or have lost. This fruitless way of thinking starts the downward cycle of negativity that repels the uplifting powers of happiness.
Instead, use the gift of appreciation to keep your attention on everything you have. We only have the present moment. Yesterday is the past. Think about the present moment and take advice from mindfulness instructors.

3. Put an end to the cycle of ingrained helplessness

To continue practicing learned helplessness is to continue to be pulled toward poverty. When the words "I can't" take up emotional and karmic space in your mind, you cannot draw wealth or other beneficial things into your life. Stop making excuses for what you cannot do and say, "I can." In other words, because I deserve happiness, I may attract prosperity.

4. Eliminate jealousy

Envy of another person's material possessions indicates that you are preoccupied with an illusion in your thoughts. Someone may not necessarily have money or be wealthy just because they drive a luxury vehicle. Jealousy is a liar because it fabricates stories virtually never based on reality. Make way for joy by letting go of your jealousies.

Remove any bad energy. Accept the straightforward things in life, and you will find peace.

5. Appreciate money's influence
The result of your labor and hard work is money. You insult yourself when you disrespect money. Keeping your finances structured is a sign of respect. That entails regularly tracking it. It involves realizing that money has both constructive and destructive potential and should not be treated carelessly.
When managed wisely, money has the potential to increase and provide for you for a very long time. When disregarded, it atrophy and harms your future. Lastly, valuing money involves avoiding using it as a flimsy method of boosting self-esteem by engaging in unnecessary spending.

6. Study money.

To attract riches into your life, you must move past wishful thinking. It entails consciously studying everything you can about money and creating means. Study the attitudes, convictions, and routines of wise people who have drawn money. They are your professors.

Understand that those genuinely wealthy don't drive fancy cars, wear designer clothing, or wear flashy jewelry. Most millionaires are careful money managers who have accumulated their wealth over decades.

7. Disburse money.

The influence of money, both spiritually and karmically, is addressed in the final point. We are recharging the human spirit when we donate money to others who are less fortunate. Money will leave you if you hoard it.

Instead, use your empathic skills to identify how you may assist those in need. An illustration would be to offer to pay for the family in need in front of you's groceries at the check out. It could also entail giving your time, which counts as money, to your preferred charity.

Giving to others out of sincere love and compassion creates more space for happiness, which is the foundation of prosperity.

Chapter 6

Millionaire attributes to Emulate

Consider the behaviors of millionaires to see if they could assist you in achieving financial success.

The most effective strategy to become a self-made millionaire is to take advice from those who have previously achieved it. As you can see, these self-made billionaires' routines are relatively simple to adopt in your day-to-day life. Because becoming a millionaire requires conserving money and investing it like you are rich rather than living like you are rich.

Hard work is required to become a self-made millionaire, but with the help of this list, you will undoubtedly be headed in the right direction for seven figures.

Six Millionaire Characteristics You Can Adopt

1. Independent Thought

The opinions of millionaires differ, including everything, not just money. Millionaires invest the time and effort everyone else expends trying to fit in by forging their path.

People should think in a way that will help them achieve their objective of wealth since thoughts influence actions. Independent thinking means having the guts to stick with what is essential to you, not what most people do. In this case, making your path is the lesson. Instead of attempting to chase the money, let your achievement propel you toward financial rewards.

2. Creative visionaries with a positive outlook are vision millionaires. In other words, prosperous people have lofty goals and strong optimism. As a result, those who desire money should have high expectations and no fear of exploring new ground.

Bill Gates, who had a net worth of $124 billion and was the second-richest person in the world in 2021, did precisely that. The co-founder of Microsoft (NYSE: MSFT) made personal computers accessible to the general public. Gates entered the private computer industry in 1975 and clung to it until he developed Microsoft Windows in 1985. When people started bringing computers into their homes, Gates was prepared to capitalize on this new era.

Gates resigned from the Microsoft board of directors in the middle of March 2020. He serves as co-chair of the Bill & Melinda Gates Foundation, the largest private charitable organization in the world to which the pair has given Microsoft stock worth $35.8 billion. Gates is now a steadfast advocate and expert on climate change.

3. Expertise

Dennis Kimbro and Napoleon Hill, authors of Think and Grow Rich: A Black Decision, interviewed successful people to identify their shared characteristics (1992). The authors discovered that successful people concentrate on their area of specialization. Millionaires often collaborate with others to strengthen their weaker areas of expertise. Consult with friends and family if you are still determining your strengths. To improve your strong skills, use training and mentors.

4. Passion.
According to multimillionaire investment guru Warren Buffett, money is a by-product of something I enjoy doing very much. If you want what you do, it will be easier to maintain the discipline to put in long hours every day. Like bankers, individuals who work in the financial industry frequently enjoy making new deals and convincing others to finish transactions.
But, it could take some time to land your ideal career, just as it does to become a millionaire. According to Entrepreneur,

even the wealthiest millionaires require an average of eight years to reach their first million.

In addition, a lot of people suffer major failures along the route. According to a Medium.com article by Pavle Marinkovic, Warren Buffett, Steve Ballmer, the former CEO of Microsoft, and Rupert Murdoch of the Fox media empire, they committed terrible blunders before becoming successful.

Thus, if you want to be wealthy, quit doing boring things and focus on what you love instead. If you are still determining what you enjoy, try a few things and keep trying until you find them.

5. Investment.
Millionaires are prepared to give up time and money to accomplish their objectives. They are prepared to take a risk now for

the chance to perform something larger eventually. Investing is a step toward attaining significant financial rewards, which can involve purchasing assets or launching a business. Get investing right away.

6. Skill in sales

Millionaires are always putting up their ideas and convincing others to accept them. Good salespeople ignore the doubters and cynics. In other words, they don't get a negative response. Rich people are also socially adept.

To sell your idea, you must be able to interact with others. In contrast to the stereotype of a salesman, millionaires credit honesty as a key to their success. Be a trustworthy salesperson and enhance your people skills to be a millionaire.

For most people, achieving their dream of becoming a millionaire takes time. In actuality, a significant portion of the world's wealthiest people amassed their fortunes over a long period (often even generations) by making wise but frequently audacious decisions, maximizing the use of their skills, and tenaciously pursuing their goals. If there's one thing you can learn from millionaires, it's that for many of them, their wealth doesn't necessarily make them stand out from the rest of the population; instead, it's what they did to get those millions that make them stand out.

Chapter 7

Reasons to be a Millionaire.

Do you aspire to financial success?

It takes a lot of work to reach the million-dollar threshold, and only the most dedicated person prepared to pay the price can do it. Millionaire status is only for some individuals who are content to settle in life. You won't become a millionaire if you seek out "get rich quick" schemes, either. It entails excellent risk with the potential for a high payoff.
Even if it's simpler than ever to become a millionaire, only some people can do it. Many people "play it safe" or let their defenses keep them from moving forward.

Those who think they can amass a significant financial fortune should continue reading.

Why should I study how to become a millionaire? It's easy. Most people who consider or discuss becoming millionaires want to spend $1 million, not necessarily make millions. Yet, if you stop to think about it, there are many more benefits to becoming a millionaire.

1. You have much greater control over your finances.

Possessing a million dollars allows you to purchase costly automobiles and houses with ten stories. You're considering the amount of control it affords you. Everyone, including you, values having access to what you can live. You want enough money to provide your family with

the proper clothing, housing, and food. ,
you want to be able to manage your
financial constraints better. Yet, remember
that every billionaire has a sizable amount
of taxes to pay; precisely, they must
contribute 40% of their earnings.

2. Your charitable impact is more
significant.
When asked, "Why do you want to be a
millionaire," you might occasionally
consider how they might have a more
significant impact on others' lives than an
average person. Having that wealth
enables you to contribute more to society
through charitable endeavors. Even while
the temptation to keep all that money for
yourself could be substantial, you'd be
surprised at how rewarding it is to assist

others. A smile will always spread when you witness your hard-earned money save someone's life or provide for their better present and future. You learn from it as well that money is more than just a toy. You could improve someone's trajectory in life with the appropriate strategy.

3. You desire to take on more danger. Having a million dollars gives you more freedom to take chances. You also have more resources and leverage to experiment with personal ventures when you have that much money. You may launch a nonprofit organization to raise awareness of a disease that doesn't get much coverage in the media. You might also develop educational initiatives that emphasize the humanities and arts. Millionaires worldwide have built their names by

challenging the status quo and undertaking seemingly complex or improbable tasks.

4. The Power To Go After What Matters
Because it acts as the medium of trade for social interactions in society, money is essential. But many things—like family and community are more significant.
You may invest more of your time your most valuable resource into cultivating the most significant connections to you once you've attained a certain level of financial freedom.

I like thinking back on Mr. Money Mustache's personal finance blog. They concentrate on the fact that he retired in his early 30s because everyone recognizes it. While it is impressive, the fact that he retired before the birth of his child has always caught my attention.

I understand that most individuals won't be able to retire and start a family simultaneously. Still, you should marry and start a family much earlier than the average person. But it's an excellent thought.

5. Managing Your Time

Your most valuable resource is time. One minute at a time, as the fictitious philosopher Tyler Durden said, "Your life is ending."

After nearly 15 months of working from home, I recently returned to the office. While there were some benefits, such as meeting new people, working eight hours seemed very solitary just a tiny bit resembling a prison.

After you achieve financial independence, you have control over how you spend your time.

Smart people continue working. You will be free to choose any initiatives you feel are crucial. The working techniques that make sense to you can be selected. If the boss walks by, you no longer have to be chained to your desk.

If you feel that going for a long walk will be the most helpful for clearing your head, you can do it without explanation.

This independence can be had if you have enough money saved to retire, but it can also be acquired by working for yourself. Making money without a regular job opens the door to considerably more flexibility than what the 9–5 world offers.

6. You Can Inspire Others

Money provides you with the ability to inspire others. Even though most wealthy people don't make a big deal out of their fortune, they inspire others with their work behind the scenes. Thanks to money, you can devote more time to charitable activities and concentrate on worthy causes.

Those who enjoy flaunting their money continue to draw attention and encourage others, even when they pass by in a Rolls-Royce or Ferrari. Having more options offers you far more control over your life, which inspires others. Money gives you options.

7. As a result, you feel safe and at ease.

Money is the best confidence booster there is. Being wealthy gives you the impression that anything is possible.

Higher self-esteem is not the same as being able to think more logically. Most importantly, you can be who you are without considering if you can "afford" to purchase ice cream for your family.

Money's certainty may give your family "peace of mind." Most people have little to no life insurance, which means that if they pass away, their loved ones won't have enough money to pay for their final expenses and other losses.

Chapter 8

Making financial blunders that prevent you from becoming wealthy

Here, we'll examine some of the most frequent financial blunders that frequently result in severe financial difficulties for individuals. Avoiding these errors could be the difference between life and death, even if you already have financial problems.

1. Excessive and unnecessary expenditures One dollar at a time is sometimes how enormous riches are lost. Even if buying that double-mocha cappuccino, going out

to dinner, or ordering that pay-per-view movie may not seem like a huge problem, everything adds up.

You spend $1,300 annually just on dining out, which might be used to cover additional credit card, auto, or other obligations. Avoiding this error is extremely important if you're in financial difficulty; after all, every dollar will matter more than ever if you're just a few dollars away from foreclosure or bankruptcy.

2. Payments That Never Stop

Do you genuinely need the things you're paying for month after month, year after year? Items like premium gym memberships, music services, and cable television can make you pay continuously while denying you ownership of anything.

Living a leaner lifestyle can help you increase your savings and protect yourself from financial hardship when money is tight or you wish to save more.

3. Residing Off of Credit

It has become very typical to use credit cards to pay for necessities. Yet even if a rising number of people are ready to pay double-digit interest rates on petrol, food, and a variety of other products that have have been before the bill is paid in full, doing so is not a good idea from a financial standpoint. Credit card interest charges substantially increase the cost of the charged items. Using credit occasionally may result in you spending more than you make.

4. Purchasing a New Vehicle

Although only some purchasers can purchase brand-new cars outright, millions do so yearly. Yet not being able to pay cash for a new car doesn't necessarily indicate that you can't afford it. After all, having enough money for the payment differs from having enough for the vehicle.

In addition, the consumer increases the gap between the worth of the car and the amount paid for it by paying interest on a depreciating asset when they borrow money to purchase a vehicle. Even worse, many people lose money trading in their cars every two to three years.

Sometimes a person has no choice but to obtain a loan to purchase a vehicle, but how many customers require a sizable SUV? Such automobiles are pricey to purchase, insure, and fuel. It is expensive to buy an SUV unless you tow a boat or trailer or require one for work.

Consider purchasing a car that consumes less gas and costs less to maintain and insure if you need to buy one and borrow money. The cost of a vehicle can be high, and if you purchase more than you require, you may be wasting money that could be saved or applied to debt repayment.

5. Overspending on your home
More significant is sometimes better when it comes to purchasing a home. If you don't have a large family, choosing a home with 6,000 square feet would result in higher taxes, maintenance, and utility costs. Do you want to eat up such a sizable chunk of your monthly budget over the long term?

6. Use Your House Equity Like a Piggy Bank.
When you refinance and withdraw money from your house, you relinquish ownership to someone else. Refinancing may be appropriate in specific circumstances, whether you can reduce your rate or refinance to pay off debt with a higher interest rate.

Opening a home equity line of credit is the other option. As a result, you can use your home's equity much like a credit card. This could result in you paying interest. You don't need to use your home equity line of credit.

7. Making ends meet month to month
The household personal savings rate in the United States was 9.4% in June 2021.

An unexpected problem might quickly become a catastrophe if you are unprepared because many homes may live paycheck to paycheck.

Those who consistently overspend find themselves in a dangerous situation where one missed paycheck would be terrible, and they depend on every dollar they make. When an economic downturn occurs, this differs from the problem you want to be in. You will only have a few choices if this happens.

A lot of financial advisors advise you to retain three months' worth of expenses in an account that is easy to access. You can run out of money due to a job loss or economic changes, putting you in a debt accumulation cycle. Three months' worth of breathing room could mean the difference between retaining and losing your home.

8. Failure to invest for retirement
You need to put your money to work for you in the markets or through other investments that generate income to retire. A pleasant retirement is dependent on making monthly contributions to specified retirement funds.
Invest in tax-deferred retirement funds and a plan offered by your employer. Know how much risk you can take and how long it will take for your investments to grow. Work with a seasoned financial advisor to align this with your objectives.

9. Eliminating Debt With Savings
You might believe that you can keep the difference by substituting your retirement account for your debt, which is currently

costing you 19% of your income while earning 7%. Yet, it takes work.

In addition to losing the benefit of compounding, it is tough to repay those retirement savings, and you risk being charged exorbitant costs. If you approach it appropriately, borrowing from your retirement account may be an option. Still, even the most diligent planners need help putting money aside to rebuild these funds.

The urgency to repay the debt typically disappears once it has been paid off. You might get back into debt since it will be very tempting to keep spending at the same rate. If you want to pay off your debt with savings, you must continue to live as though you still owe your retirement fund money.

10. Making no plans

What happens now will have an impact on your financial future. Spending two hours a week on finances is unthinkable for many who spend countless hours watching TV or browsing through their social media accounts. Where you are going must be known. Make it a duty to take the time to plan your finances.

Start keeping an eye on the minor expenses that add up quickly to avoid the risks of overspending, then go on to keep an eye on the higher costs. Consider your options carefully before adding any more debt to your list of obligations, and remember that just because you can make a payment doesn't mean you can afford the item. Finally, prioritize saving a portion of your income each month and creating a solid financial plan.

Conclusion

Even though schemes to become rich quickly occasionally may seem alluring, the tried-and-true method of accumulating wealth is via consistent saving and investing and patiently waiting for that money to grow over time. Starting little is acceptable. Starting early and consistently is crucial. Make money, save it, and then wisely invest it. Insurance can help you safeguard your assets while reducing your tax liability.

Understand that accumulating wealth is a process rather than a final goal.

Throughout the road, celebrate your accomplishments and resist the urge to give up because of setbacks or difficulties. You can succeed financially and accumulate wealth over time if you have patience, discipline, and a clear understanding of your objectives.

When you decide to quit putting obstacles in your path, accumulating wealth becomes much more straightforward. Set yourself free today and begin collecting the fortune you have always desired.